To Jessica & Family

Good Souls Short Stories

Written by

Paul Wine

Paul

Published by BCD Advisors

Princeton, New Jersey

www.BCDadvisors.com
info@BCDadvisors.com

Edited by Ross Wayne

Copyright 2013 by
Paul Wine

All rights reserved. No part of this book may be reproduced without consent from the authors or publisher.

Paperback ISBN 978-1-60970-041-6

Other BCDadvisors "Teach to Fish" Books

Good-Spirited Short Stories

Maximum Backgammon

Power Baby's Life Adventures

Nina Nasturtium Teaches Biology

Baseball + Numbers = Fun & Games

Dedication

I dedicated my first book, "Good-Spirited Short Stories," to all good-spirited people – and especially Albert Schweitzer, who received a Noble Peace Prize for his good works.

There have been other people in my life that never received Noble Peace Prizes for their good works – yet have done good in my life. One of these persons was Theresa Garone, a woman who treated me like her son; I reciprocated, as I treated her like my mother for over 35 years. Another was Dr. David Cory, my pastor for about 30 years – a man who kept me on the straight and narrow. These two people are not in the world any longer, but there are many people in my life – too many to name – who helped me to create good- spirited stories. Thanks to all those people. Remember, that in one's life, it takes many people to make good stories – that make life worthwhile

- Paul Wine

Acknowledgements

As in my first book, "Good- Spirited Short Stories," I acknowledge Homecrest Community Services, Inc. for providing the platform for my story writing – because I wrote my first stories for my senior adult day program. All the people that have read my "Good-Spirited Short Stories" inspired this new book of stories. They so enjoyed my book, which gave me greatest of joy – and the will to write more stories. Thanks to my family and friends – especially Eunice He and Ben Bruen – who have made my life good enough to create good stories.

I would also like to thank Ross Wayne for editing this book and Carlton Chin for their work in getting this book published. Thanks also to BCDadvisors for publishing this book.

- Paul Wine

Table of Contents

Dedication 4
Acknowledgements 5
Table of Contents 7
A Note from the Author 9
Part 1: Humorous & Nice Stories 11
    The Singer 13
    The Dentist 21
    The Wallpaper Man 27
    The Miracle Baby 31
    The Pop-Up King 35
    The Actor 41
Part 2: Lessons 47
    The Preacher 49
    The Mirror 55
    Losing My Marbles 61
    Hairy 65
    The Storyteller 71
    Sanity Clause 77
Part 3: Observations 85
    The Lover 87
    The Invisible Man 93
    The Dancer 99
    The Bully 103
    The Ad Man 109
    Seeing Clearly 115
    My Golden Teeth 119
    Looking Up 123

A Note from the Author

In my first book, I mentioned that I love to keep watch on the political life of the world and that I hoped that my kind of political life – such as peace, environmental sanity, true human rights, and true democracy – would one day be the guiding force of life. All of these aspects of life are a passion of mine. I have worked for the peace movement and the environmental movement. I try not to waste my vote. I give money to "Democracy Now," a news program that gives truth to the news and "TomDispatch," a news website that keeps one up on the US in the world. Information is vital to citizens of this country – so that a country of the people, by the people, and for the people – can make decisions for this country. I hope that everyone who is reading my book understands that peace and environmental peace is far away. It will take the billions of people on this planet to make a true effort to protect life and the planet. Greed and elitist power are ruling human life now – and that must change in order for human life to survive.

I write very light stories. None of the violence of the day, reported by our news outlets – or deep, dark, conflicting pain that people go through – are the main themes of my stories. One of my friends reviewed my first book and said, "These stories of author Paul Wine are the opposite of victim lit. They are insight lit." The stories I have written are good-natured. I know that the world keeps us from much of the good nature we possess – that is necessary for our families and ourselves – to live in peace and harmony with nature. These stories hopefully (even though they are fantasy, having some hidden reality to them) – will highlight people's better nature. This can help to create the will and actions needed to save this world from falling apart – especially global warming, which threatens all humanity. I hope that this book, "Good Souls Short Stories," will be read by the good souls that have read my first book and help inspire a long story for humanity of peace and environmental sanity. My soul pleads to God – and pleads that humanity – will wake up, so we can all have good stories to tell.

Good Soul
Paul Wine

Brooklyn, NY
November 22, 2013

Part 1: Humorous & Nice Stories

The Singer

Richard was a shy, shy, shy man. He was so shy everyone who knew him could hardly believe that he found a wife. However, needing love helped him overcome his shyness. Richard led a quiet life, working in the post office – in the personnel-filing department. Although he realized that his shyness kept him from getting a better position, he was content with his life. He was also a very good singer – as he learned to sing as a child in his church choir. Now, as an adult, his shyness kept him from singing in public. He did love to sing, so he would sing only in the shower. His wife loved his singing. She listened at the bathroom door and if she requested a song for him, Richard would learn – it doing his best to sing it well. She always wished others could hear him sing, because she believed Richard was an exceptional singer.

One night, their neighbors came over to their backyard to enjoy relaxing conversation with one other. Well, Richard took an early shower and as the bathroom was on the first floor, the neighbors heard Richard singing – which they thoroughly enjoyed. Debbie was proud of her husband, as the neighbors praised him. Since Richard was not a social man, she never had the chance to show him off; he was also a handsome and kindly man. Night after night, during the summer, Debbie got her husband to take his shower early. She gave him a list of songs that she wanted him to sing – which he loved to do for her. It seemed like a simple request to make his wife happy. Night after night, her friends came for the show. They all kept this a secret from Richard because they were certain that if he knew they were listening, he would stop – and they really loved his singing style.

One night, change was in the air, as a neighbor brought a music producer over to Debbie's backyard to hear this strange, yet enjoyable singer. The music producer loved Richard's voice and wanted to produce a CD. Debbie thanked the man and said that Richard would never consent to such a thing. The producer, understanding the strange situation, offered to record Richard without him knowing. It could be recorded as he showered – and the noise of the water would be removed. Debbie thought it would be great for her husband to make a record but wondered how to keep him in the dark. The producer said that he would not use Richard's name – but instead, would just call him "The Singer." The neighbors agreed to keep it a secret, as they did not want to lose their private concerts.

The record producer turned Richard's bathroom into a recording studio without him knowing. Debbie said that she just wanted to do a complete makeover of the bathroom. As usual, Debbie continued to give Richard a list of songs she wanted him to sing. A CD was produced, which sold fairly well. No name was listed – as to who the singer was; the CD was simply called "The Singer." Debbie was very happy because they could use the extra money. However, she had to tell her husband that the monies came from a relative's will. She was also worried because she did not know how her husband would react if he found out about his new career. A second album was created which sold very well; Richard was becoming famous without being known.

Due to the success of the second album, the record producer wanted Richard to do a concert. Debbie was totally against this because she knew her husband would never sing to an audience – and he would find out what she had done. The record producer had an idea. On stage, the audience would just see a shower in which Richard would sing and use this strange idea to gain interest in this novelty act. She still said, "No," – but the record producer had a contract that she signed that called for her husband to do a concert if he had a successful CD, which was in the fine print. Debbie panicked because she thought that if her husband ever found out, he might leave her – and she loved him so much. The producer felt that they could have their cake and eat it too – as he was sure that he could rig up a shower in Madison Square Garden. Richard would think it was a shower in a hotel room. She went along with the idea; not only was it in the contract, but having her husband sing in Madison Square Garden was a thrill.

The night of the concert came and Debbie was excited and worried – but she tried to show no emotions as she steered her husband to his shower. She brought him to a suite and asked him to serenade her as she had something important to tell him. She gave him a list of songs that the recorder producer wanted him to sing. Richard knew his wife very well and if she said that, she had something important to tell him it would be important and he sang with vigor – anticipating some good news.

The audience at the Garden went wild, as not only was the singing very good but the singer was behind a frosted glass wall in a shower and the singer was singing as he was taking a shower. They applauded and laughed loudly and hoped to find out who this mystery singer was… In their anticipation, a rumor got out that indeed, they would find out who this singer was. He would come out at the end of the concert and he would tell them why he sang in secret. Debbie saw the crowd behind the stage and thought that it would be wonderful if Richard could know he had so many fans. However, she knew he would be shocked and devastated if he knew he was famous. She thought she could never let him know.

After the "concert" Richard gave for his wife in the shower, he dried off and asked her just what was so important that she wanted him to sing for an hour. She told him that what she was about to say was a life changing event; she told him that she was with child. Richard could not have been happier as it was their first, they hugged and he felt they were ready to start a new family together.

Meanwhile, in the concert hall, it was the end of the concert and the house lights came on.

However, there was no singer. The audience really wanted to see the singer and started to get angry when they were told that the concert was over and the singer already said, "Good night." The crowd felt betrayed, started to boo, and left the Garden with the resolution to never listen to The Singer again. A CD of the "The Singer, Live at the Garden," did not sell well. Debbie felt that this ending was probably a good thing – because she did not enjoy fooling her husband.

Richard's career in singing began and ended strangely. However, Debbie knew her husband was special – even if he did not know his hidden life and how truly special he was. In addition, without his knowing, he provided for their new family very handsomely as the singing he did do, paid very well.

Many months later, Debbie had their baby a girl, which both parents doted over. Richard wanted to create a picture album, so he rummaged through the closet for an album for his pictures. He found an album with articles in it already – which he had never seen before. The articles were about "The Singer," an entertainer that he had heard about at the water cooler. He dismissed this entertainer because his wife never talked about, "The Singer" – and she would have, if this singer were any good. However, why would she keep such an album? A CD was in the picture album, which said that this person was just too shy to let the public know who he was. Richard wanted to hear this CD and played it. To his amazement, he heard himself singing. This was just as magical and wonderful as having a child. He laughed and could not understand how this happened. I am "The Singer," he thought.

To her horror, Debbie came into the room for a jacket and saw her husband looking at the album and listening to the CD. She was very scared. Meekly, she spoke, saying that she could explain – to which he said, "I hoped you would."

Trembling, she told him the whole amazing story, which he listened to – without showing any emotion. Bursting with fear, she asked him what he thought. He laughed and bear-hugged his wife.

He thought that this was the greatest thing to ever happen to him – except his child, of course. She cried, as keeping this secret from him had its toll. He was happy about it and she wondered why. He said that he loved to sing but he would never have been able to sing had he known about the CD and the concert. She had made him famous without telling him – but more importantly, with nobody else knowing. It would be very painful for him if the public knew and she told him there was a clause in the contract to keep his identity a secret. The only problem is that some of her friends knew and would not tell – as long as they could still hear him at night, as he showered. Richard agreed, as long as he did not have to socialize with her friends. He wanted to keep his "cover" as an office worker.

Going back to work with this new knowledge of himself, his coworkers could see something had changed with Richard but they could not tell what. This was somewhat normal – because his coworkers never seemed to know just what Richard was thinking, because he was always so shy. Richard thought that being the person he was – he was so lucky that he had everything he wanted: a loving wife, a child, and fame – which no one knew about, which was just fine for him. As he filed his papers, he felt like a child joyously fantasying about fame, doing all those things the rich and famous do. Yet he was famous and he was doing just what his personality allowed him to do – as keeping it secret was the only real way he could handle fame. He now had a great deal of satisfaction with his life and even if it only in his head he would be forever, "The Singer."

The Dentist

Jim, as a young boy, found a great deal of interest in his teeth. When his baby teeth came, he wanted his mother to measure them every day – to see how fast they were growing. She humored him and they made a chart of his baby teeth to chart the growth of his teeth. He was sad to learn that these baby teeth would fall out, yet he was looking forward to his permanent teeth.

Jim also was interested in other's teeth. He was fond of putting his fingers into the mouths of his friends – to see their teeth, which left their mothers very unhappy. Jim saw on a movie of a tooth being pulled out. A string was tied to both the tooth and a doorknob; then, by shutting the door the tooth was pulled. He would have to try it. Eventually, one of his baby teeth became loose and he tied his tooth to the door and had his friend shut the door pulling the tooth out. However, a lot of blood came out of his mouth and he yelled for his mother. His mother stopped the bleeding and told him he must stop this unhealthy curiosity of his teeth. Now, he had good reason to listen to her.

He lost some interest in playing dentist, at least with his own teeth and played many other boyish games with his friends. Jim still had an interest in dentistry. When he went to the dentist, he would ask the dentist all sorts of questions about being a dentist – and about all the tools involved in the job. He saw the tooth mirror and knew he had to have one so he could look at his friends' teeth. He figured he could con the doctor to let him use it. He told the doctor that he had a career day at school and he thought that dentistry would be his interest. Jim said that some tools to show at school would make a good presentation. He asked the doctor how to use the dental mirror and what to look for when looking at a tooth – to get a good idea of what to say at career day.

The dentist, seeing his interest was flattered and gave Jim an old dental as a souvenir. He told Jim not to use it on himself or others – as it had to be sterilized first. Jim was getting just what he wanted and of course, agreed not to use it – "Just a small con," Jim thought.

As soon as he could, Jim played dentist with his friends. He sterilized the mirror with alcohol and looked at all his friend's teeth – really looking to see if he could spot a problem tooth. His friends played along with Jim to a point but they got bored with Jim playing dentist and went to play other games – and so did Jim.

Jim was not a very good student and just barely passed his studies at high school. He would not be going to college if he did not study. Jim just did not have any interest in his studies and his parents wondered what was to become of him. Jim told his parents that his only interest was dentistry and maybe the family dentist could mentor him. Then, he might pass his tests to become a dentist. The family dentist mentored Jim and showed him the basics of dentistry, which Jim enjoyed. However, it was not enough motivation to get good grades in high school. Jim just made the passing grade to graduate – but not good enough for college – which he kept from his parents. He had to con them and try to figure how to do what he truly wanted to do with his life, which was dentistry.

A friend told Jim about a free dentist clinic where students did the work under supervision of a dentist. Jim was able to con the dentist into thinking that he was a student, and learned as much and as fast as he could – before he was caught. He learned to fill teeth, pull teeth, clean teeth – and was going to learn how to make false teeth, when a fellow student told him he had been uncovered. Jim left in a hurry, never to be found by the clinic, to face the music.

Jim still needed to learn more if he was to try to become a dentist without formal training. He found trade shows where dental companies would informally train dentists on their products. He learned how to use the newest material to make false teeth – which was demonstrated to him. The sales person let him use the material on a dummy. He felt that he was on his way to pulling off the con of being a bona fide dentist.

He printed out a phony diploma, making him, in his eyes – a dentist. His parents could not have been prouder and he used them to get the money to set up an office because the bank would never fall for his con. Therefore, he set up a practice, which he was very happy about. This would be his life's work. His clients were happy as well because he was very gentle and patient. He did have trouble making false teeth; it usually took him two times to get it right, but he did not charge that much. Most patients overlooked this lack of skill, as he was very personable.

Jim did have some tough customers and one of them was Mr. Worth who was very unhappy with his dentures. Even after the second time, they did not fit correctly. He wondered just what school Jim went to and read the diploma closely to see the school name. Mr. Worth was going to complain to the school but found out there was not any such school. He discovered that Jim was a fraud. Mr. Worth was very angry at being conned, so he brought criminal case against Jim. The judge thought that it was very dangerous that anyone would impersonate a professional person. Jim defended himself, as he had done no harm; he just helped people. He did not have a license because his grades at school were not good enough for dentistry school. It was the love of my life and he learned the trade through other ways. He went on to say that not only did he do good enough work, but his fees were very low. The judge took that into account, but Jim had broken the law and Jim was sentenced to two years in prison. He was ordered never to do dentistry again. Jim was heartbroken, but off to prison he went.

In prison, he was very unhappy. However, his parents' visits brought not only themselves – but many letters from the people he worked on, hoping to see him soon – and how unfair that he was doing time. One day, in prison, his life turned around. The warden called him into his office and told him that the prison's dentist quit. There was not much money to pay a new dentist and he knew from his file that he was an uncertified dentist.

The warden then asked him if he would do the dentistry, as it was greatly needed for the inmates. He was pleased to do what he loved the most in the entire world – and so he became the "cons' dentist." The cons loved the work he did and Jim became well respected in the prison. However, what would he do when he got home? The day came when he was to leave and he was very unhappy. He knew this was strange – because he would be free – but free to do what?

Jim thought he was just a "con artist dentist" and a "dentist for cons" – and being a dentist was all he ever wanted to do. Before Jim left for the free world, the warden thanked him for his service. The warden asked if for a small salary – if Jim would continue to work as the prison's dentist. The warden said the state would look the other way as to his education – because he was desperate to get a good dentist. Jim could not have been happier. Now, Jim would be able do the work he loved, knowing in his heart and now being known as, "The Dentist."

The Wallpaper Man

My father was a hard worker and a good provider for our family. He was a wallpaper hanger and very good at it and so we called him the wallpaper man. He seemed to love his work, which I did not totally understand – as I wanted to be an artist. However, my father wanted me to keep my eyes on the ground and follow him into being a wallpaper hanger. During summer breaks, we worked together – and I worked so I could get supplies for my artwork. I found the work physically hard and my hands would get sticky with paste – which I felt was beneath my artist hands. I carried my sketchpad everywhere I went. My favorite thing was to draw patterns. I looked at cracks in walls, floors, sidewalks and created patterns from what I saw – as they were always different. I studied tree bark and even broken glass and from these patterns, I created what I thought were unique patterns. I knew it was not great art, but it was a beginning, which pleased me to no end.

After high school, I had the grades – and enough sketches – to be accepted into an art school, which my father hated. He did pay for it, as he did love me –and he figured that after I got this "art bug" out of my system, I would be working with him. I worked hard at art school. I painted and drew everything my teachers wanted me to: from nudes to apples. In painting class, I learnt the many different colors that good art was made of, which I incorporated in my patterns. I was happiest during free time – when I was sketching deigns – sometimes from lines on my friend's hands. Sketching patterns was the art (at least what I called art) I loved the best, but there was no class for that. Some of my teachers liked my patterns but did not see the artistic value of them. One teacher said I had promise. However, although my sketches were pretty, the teacher said they were not something someone would buy to hang up in their living room.

Upon graduation, I left with good grades, meaning that I could do fine art. I felt that I should be able to create very valuable art works but I had not created any major work: just normal fare, as far as art is concerned. My father called me the "artist" and took me back to work with him so I would not be a starving artist. He saw my art education as pie in the sky, but I kept my dream alive. I still carried my sketchbook wherever I went – and I would create more deigns. I was disappointed with myself but I believed I would do something with my talent and education someday.

One day my father brought me to wallpaper manufacturing plant, which turned out to be fascinating. I never really looked at wallpaper before. It was always just paper that needed to be put up on a wall – which was dull work for me, dulling my senses. I looked at all of the wallpaper products and saw the many different colors and designs on them. I had never seen so many; they looked like art to me. My father introduced me to the foreman and I told him I thought that the wallpaper looked like art. I said that I was an artist and showed him my sketchbook. He looked at the sketchbook and sent me to the office where there were men who created the new and different designs of wallpaper. They liked my designs, and much to my surprise, they hired me on the spot as an apprentice. It was a trial period to see if I could create new and appealing wallpaper designs. After a few years I became very good at creating wallpaper, so much so that I became famous in the wallpaper line. I had my own line of wallpaper that sold throughout the country. My teachers did not see the value of my art, yet I always did – and now my art, on wallpaper, was hanging on people's walls all throughout the USA.

    Becoming a successful artist, in my own way, is one of my great pleasures. However, my greatest pleasure is my father being so proud of me that he now calls me, "The Wallpaper Man."

The Miracle Baby

Jane was her name. She was my only baby girl that I fretted over constantly. I called her my "miracle baby" because I was in my forties when I gave birth to my lovely baby Jane. At the age of two, she had not spoken a word – not even, "Momma or papa," which greatly worried me. I went to a speech specialist to see about her problem. The doctor said that it was probably that she was just a late bloomer. He gave me a few books with pictures and words and wanted me to do the exercises in the books with her and come back in a few weeks to see if she was able to make any sounds that sounded like the simple words in the books.

I did exercises every day with Jane to no avail. However, the exercises brought about the beginning of the strangeness of my baby. I held a dime in my fingers and said to my daughter, "Coin," which I repeated a few times. Her first word was "coin."

I was so happy that I hugged my baby and it seemed that two dimes fell from my hands. I figured that I must be dreaming about the second coin and I did not care, as Jane said her first word. For days, she did not say anything else and I was disappointed, but I kept trying. I took her favorite doll and repeated, "Doll," many times, and then it happened. She said the word, "Doll," and magically, a duplicate doll appeared in my hand.

When my husband came home from work, I told him what had happened and he just shrugged it off saying that I was dreaming. I wanted to prove to him that Jane was a miracle baby and I took my one-of-a-kind antique mirror and said to my baby, "Mirror," many times.

Lo and behold, she said, "Mirror," and an exact copy was in front of me and I could not tell them apart. When my husband came home, I showed him the proof of what I had been saying and he was aghast. He got his favorite hat and said "hat" many times to Jane. Jane said "hat" and he had a duplicate. He was so happy that he wanted to share Jane our miracle baby with the world. I was not so sure I wanted her to be famous.

My husband got my baby on a TV show called, "People's Amazing Feats." On the show, my husband took the host's eyeglasses and repeated the word "glasses" to my baby and the baby said "glasses" and in my husband's hand were identical glasses. The host was amazed, yet all in the audience thought it was a trick. We knew it was not a trick.

We were invited to many places to perform my baby's miracles, which we did – making us quite famous. People demanded to know the truth about baby Jane, as my baby did not speak and only said the word we gave her only once. People thought it must be a trick and we should be exposed as fakers.

We went into a studio where we would be on a world broadcast with all the greatest magicians in the world – to find out if my baby was indeed a miracle baby. They gave my husband a ten-dollar bill, which was fresh from the United States Mint and asked to see if the baby could make an exact duplicate. I was sure this would prove that she was not a fake. Well, my husband held the bill up to Jane and repeated the word "bill" and in no time at all she said bill, and a duplicate with the exact serial number on it appeared. They were all satisfied that Jane could produce miracles, and all the world's politicians wanted us to visit them as I am sure they wanted the magic to rub off on them.

The big day arrived when we were to meet with the President of the United States. We stood in wonder as we were escorted into the White House and into the Oval Office where we were face-to-face with the President. My husband and I shook hand with the President and he asked if my baby could perform a miracle for him. I agreed, but first I wanted a picture of my family and him – so I held my baby up in front of the President and told my baby to smile for the President. Jane said, "Thank you, Mr. President," and another one of miracles happened. Now, next to me was an identical President. Now there were two Presidents – and some people in the room screamed and some fainted. Security came after me and my baby. I ran out of the room and out of the White House to the White House lawn. Outside, there was an army of soldiers with guns pointing at me and my baby. I was so scared that I just sat down on the lawn and started to cry, holding my baby.

The next thing I knew, I was covered in sweat and my husband was waking me up and said that I must have had a bad dream as I was saying, "Please don't hurt her." I looked around and sure enough, I was in my bed and my "miracle baby story" was just a dream. Yet now, I had to get up just to see my baby who was lying in bed – and seeing me, she started to giggle. I picked her up lovingly and said that she should never worry, as mommy will always be here for you. In addition, lo and behold – my baby said, "Mommy," her first word, and now I knew that she was truly my miracle baby.

The Pop-Up King

Eric loved baseball and dreamt of becoming a professional player, but his play needed work. His glove work was very good but he was a disaster at hitting. He usually hit a pop-up when it was his time at bat. His best friend, Billy, worked hard with him on his hitting. After a summer of trying, Billy gave up – as every game they played, Eric would hit a pop-up. However, he was becoming a very good infield player as he could play any infield position. Eric's friends let Eric play with them because he was so good on the field. However, they laughingly called him the "pop-up king" because he only had pop-up appearances at the plate.

After a few summers of playing ball with his friends and seeing his lack of hitting ability, Eric still wanted to play professional so he joined a little league team. The team's hitting coach worked hard with Eric. Soon, Eric was able to hit ground balls – which he hoped would lead to a hit: something that had eluded him so far. Eric played hard and his teammates respected that, yet every time he came to bat, he hit a pop up and his "pop up king" nickname seemed to suit him. Eric would be pulled out of a game by the manager any time the team needed a hit and he was up. On the other hand, Eric saved many a game using his glove. Eric saw that his glove was a major asset to the team and practiced hard at playing all of the infield positions. The manager played Eric at all the infield positions at different times. All of his teammates thought that he should get a golden glove for his excellent play in the field. Eric saw that his dream of playing for a major league team would probably remain a dream because he just could not hit the ball – other than a pop-up.

Eric went to college to find a career but he was able to play some baseball on the college team. His play in the field just got better and better. He was becoming a star shortstop but he still could not hit the ball. While he was playing college baseball, the hitting coach made him practice and practice his hitting – but to no avail. The fans of the college team would always laugh when he came to bat and yell for the opposing team to drop the ball. No one could believe that a ball player would only hit pop-ups and people came out to see the pop-up king. Eric would hit pop-ups so high that he could run to third base before the ball was caught. Eric always hoped that the opposing fielder would drop the ball, so even if it were an error, he would be on base. However, there was no such luck. Eric truly loved to play baseball even though that he not only could not hit but he was becoming a good-natured joke. The crowds would laugh at his at bat – making Eric very unhappy. Eric studied hard at college, thinking that he would go into computer software – since baseball seemed out of the question. At the end of his four years in college and playing for the college team, a scout asked him if he wanted to join the Tigers' minor league team. The scout knew his trouble with hitting but he was sure that their coaches could get him to hit. Eric said, "Yes," as baseball was his only true love and he truly felt that someday he would be able to hit.

Eric joined the Tigers' minor league team with the hope that someday he would be able to play in the majors. However, he knew that he needed to overcome his hitting problem. He trained with the coaches to overcome his problem, but it only seemed to get worse. He swung harder and the ball would just pop up higher. Every at bat, Eric would pray that the ball was not caught, but of course, there was no such luck. The manager played him, as his glove at shortstop was so very good. However, as in the past, if a situation arose that called for a hit, Eric would be pulled out of the game. Eric had his problems, yet he was becoming famous with the fans as the pop-up king. He was so famous, that he had his own fan club, so to speak. His fans would yell joyfully, "Pop-up!" every time he went to the plate. This angered him a bit, as they were celebrating his weakness. At times, he hit the ball so hard that it popped-up, foul, out of the stadium – which the fans loved. Eric's manager wished that there was a "designated fielder" position because Eric was truly a great shortstop fielder – and he would be able to play him all the time. One day, to Eric's great joy, he was called up to the majors as the Tigers' shortstop was injured during the playoffs.

The Tigers had a very good hitting team and defense at shortstop in the playoffs was vital – so Eric would get to play. It was during the last game of the league championship playoffs that Eric shined. The bases were loaded with no outs. The Tigers could lose the game and a line drive was headed over second base. Eric jumped as high as he could and caught the ball on a fly, stepped on second – and threw to first – completing a triple play. The fans went wild, as that was the end of the threat – and now the Tigers were headed to the World Series.

Eric could not have been happier – to not only help get the Tigers into the World Series, but to be there himself. It was a dream come true. During the World Series, the Tigers played the Mets, which was expected to be a very close and hotly contested series. Eric played the field during the late innings for defense, but anytime a hit was needed, he would be pulled. It came down to the seventh game and Eric was put into the game in the ninth inning. The game was tied 1-1 and it went into extra innings. Many extra innings. It went to the seventeenth inning and all the players on the bench had been used on both sides. In the top of the seventeenth, the Mets had scored a run to go ahead in the game. If the Tigers did not get at least a run in the bottom of the seventeenth, they would lose the game. In the bottom of the seventeenth inning, Eric came up to bat with two outs and a man on third. The manager had no one on the bench to bat for Eric so he told him not to swing. The only hope he had was for Eric to get a walk. Eric went to bat praying for a walk as the game came down to him getting on base – so the next batter could get a winning hit. If he did not get a walk, it would be the end of the game – and perhaps the end of his baseball career. Eric got up to bat and he watched strike one go by; then strike two. The next pitch could end the game, which he could not let happen. The next pitch was coming right down the middle of the plate. He knew it would be strike three, so he swung with all his might and hoped to hit the ball. Eric of course hit a pop-up but so high that it went out of the lights of the stadium into a cloudy night and the infielders did not know where it was, so Eric just ran the bases. The infielders thought that he might have hit it out of the stadium but then they saw a white object coming out of the lights near third base as Eric rounded third. The infielders ran to third but it was a dove flying into the stadium. The ball came down fast and fell near first base. The first baseman ran to first, picked up the ball, and threw home but it was too late as Eric touched home plate safely. Eric had hit the first ever pop-up home run winning the game, which might put him in the Hall of Fame. The fans and the Tigers were laughing with tears in their eyes, as they were now able to have a great celebration. Eric knew that this was the greatest moment in his baseball career – and that nothing could top it. He decided that this would be his last game and he would be proud to now be called, "The Pop-Up King."

The Actor

As a child, I loved to act. I would play doctor, Indian, cowboy – and even take my father's briefcase – and play businessperson. At family gatherings, there was always a good audience. They would always ask me what I was going to be when I grew up. I would just shrug my shoulders and they would laugh with a knowing eye; they believed that I might become an actor.

Well, seeing that my family thought I might become an actor, I tried some roles in my church plays. I once played Joseph, Jesus' dad for a Christmas play – and found it very unsatisfying, as it seemed very unreal. An actor should be seen as the "genuine article" to be truly acting. I tried some other plays at church, but all the roles seemed unreal because everyone knew it was me playing the role. It seemed to me that acting does not allow one to be seen as the actual person one is playing, so it is just a phony art. I put my childhood dream away, went off to college, and became an accountant.

Many years passed and I was in a new church and the pastor became sick just before a Sunday service. The congregation went on with the service as the pastor wished – but the pastor was too sick to give the sermon. At that moment, I was overcome with the acting bug and I stood up and told the congregation that I was a pastor from the next town over and I would love to give the sermon. They were happy that a pastor was among them and agreed to let me give the sermon. I gave quite a performance and the sermon was a success. I greeted everyone at the door as they were leaving and they felt blessed to have me that Sunday.

"Now this was real acting," I thought, as I left the church, as nobody knew who I really was and everyone saw me as a real preacher. My next opportunity to act came, as I was to audit high school accounts. I was waiting in the main office and I overheard that they were short of a math teacher that day. Therefore, I told the person in charge that I was also a math teacher and I could substitute, as the audit could wait. They let me and I taught math all day long and it was great. All of the students called me, "Teach," and playing the teacher, I even taught them math. I had them all thinking that I was a real teacher because of my acting ability, I believed. I left and told the main office that I would be in touch about my teacher's license and how to pay me and they were okay with that. I walked away a very happy man since acting was very exciting and my normal job was not.

The next day I had a dentist appointment. I walked into the office and the dental assistant asked me if I could watch the office because she had to run an errand. She said she would not be long and the dentist was running late but they would be able to see me in about fifteen minutes. I said, "Fine."

When she left, I went into the dentist room, found his white smock, and put it on, feeling as if I was a dentist. A woman walked into the room looking for anybody and she said, "Hi, doc." She asked me to examine her and I did as if I was a dentist. She said she had no current problems that this was just a checkup. I gave her a clean bill of health but told her to come back at a later date to get a cleaning by my dental assistant. She left and the dental assistant came back and I excused myself, saying that I needed to get back to work and I would reschedule. It again felt great to be an actor, I thought.

Now that I had put on a costume for a role, I decided for my next role, to buy a crossing guard's outfit so I would have the authority to get children across the street safely. I started the next morning and was greeted by happy children and their parents going to their schools and they were glad that I was there crossing them. They acknowledged my first day on the job and that this was the first time that the street I covered had a crossing guard and that it was needed. It was so much fun that I went back in the afternoon as school let out and that is where my troubles began.

Two police officers came up to me and asked me for my crossing guard ID. I told them I must have left it at home and I would bring it tomorrow when I came to work. They did not like that idea and were suspicious of me as this was a street that never had a crossing guard. At the station house, I confessed to playing the role of crossing guard as the acting bug had taken hold of me. I told them of the other roles that I recently played thinking that they might be impressed. Instead, they arrested me as a con man; I was flabbergasted and got a lawyer to defend me.

I went in front of a judge and my lawyer explained to the judge that I was harmless and caused no harm to anyone and that I truly believed that I was just acting. The judge asked me if what my lawyer said was true and I said I thought I was just acting like any other actor on the movie screen or TV. The judge said that since I had such trouble seeing reality that he ordered me to counseling and to do community service by helping a community theater group and to go see real acting. I agreed but didn't see the reason for the great fuss. My local paper picked up my arrest and titled an article called "The Actor" about me and my "Acting" career. People in my small town saw my picture in the article which basically called me a conman and now people behind my back whispered there goes "the Actor" causing me a great deal of pain,

I went to see the counselor to help me overcome my problems. I told him I thought that true acting was where somebody was accepted as another without knowing it was not true. He explained to me that my concept of acting was deceitful. Real actors play a role that the audience knows is not real yet the audience suspends belief so that they see the actor as if the person they are portraying is real. He said that spending time with the community theater group would help me understand. I agreed to try to understand and I would never act like I had done in the past but could I go to a new town, as my name was now mud here. The judge and the counselor agreed.

I went to the new town and during the day, I did accounting and my nights were spent in the court-ordered community theater where I was to learn what was "normal" acting was. I started working on the sets, building, painting and doing sound checks. I watched the actors create their roles with the works from the play and with much work, they were believable to me. The audience always appreciated the actors who totally convinced them of the people they were playing as it made the play so engrossing. I wanted to try my hand at this kind of acting and they gave me a part.

I found this stage acting more work to be believed than what I did previously: living a lie. Over the years, I played many different roles with this community theater and have done so quite successfully. Now I raise my head in pride when someone behind my back whispers there goes, "The Actor."

Part 2: Lessons

The Preacher

Early in life, I found that I liked to express my views – and have others see and agree with my views. My friends and family nicknamed me, "The Preacher." I preached politics, religion, economics and any opinion that I currently held. Sometimes I was a bit much for my family and my friends but I usually captured and held the attention of my audience. People thought the way I saw the world was a little wrong-headed as there was always some resistance to my ideas. Why should others see the world the way I did? I did not know why. Yet I knew it was my fate to go into the world and preach my view to people.

When I got to high school, my persuasion skills were sharp – or so I thought. I was able to gather a small crowd at lunchtime and I would always have a topic to preach on. I was having a grand time and a teacher said that I should use my talent on the debate team. I thought that was a good idea. The debating team was not as much fun as I thought – because of judgment of one's argument. In a debate, one could lose to another's point of view and I always wanted others to believe in my view. After a few losses, I quit the team. I thought that needing others to believe in my way – was possibly a little too strong. Perhaps it was even a little evil, yet it was the way I wanted to be. I kept expressing myself strongly and made friends with those who were like-minded.

After high school, I needed to decide what to do with my life. My high school counselor spent time with me. We reviewed many professions that that matched up with my grades and interests – but I knew choosing a profession would take some time. It took some soul-searching on my part. I realized that going to church and watching the preacher preach the word to the congregation – that he had the people in the palm of his hand. They took him seriously. One of the benefits of preaching God's word was that in the believer's eyes, God's words were the unquestioned truth – and I needed my words to be accepted. I also thought that preaching "the word" might be perfect because I loved to tell people what to think. To have the authority of God behind me seemed too good to be true. Therefore, I went to college and majored in religion and then went to seminary to become a preacher. I became what everyone who knew me always called me anyway, "The Preacher."

During my college years and in the seminary, I could not take religion too seriously. After years of study, I could not believe everything in the bible. I found that I was not a true believer; I saw religion as a means to an end. In fact, one night, my college friends and I drank ourselves sick. We made fun of religion and people who were believers. I was so bad that I held up the bible and shouted that I was going to preach and that I would make my friends, "Buy Bull" – a play on the word bible and religion. This caused me to do some soul searching. After I woke up the next day, I had a tremendous headache and serious questions for myself. What was I to do with my life – as an unbeliever after so many year of study?

I thought long and hard about becoming a preacher. However, even after that night, I still wanted to preach. I saw religion as a great way to get others to see a point of view. I understood that what I wanted to do seemed a little evil but I felt that religion really did no harm and could do a world of good for people.

I became a preacher. I passed all my seminary tests and convinced other religious leaders that I was called by God to preach the word. I was a phony because I did not even know if there was a God. Yet, there were believers – and those to turn into believers. They would all listen to my every word and believe – which seemed to justify my life's will, at least to myself.

Not feeling right about joining an established religious group, I started out preaching in a public park every Sunday for months. I gathered a following. Soon, we rented a building and created our own church, "The Church for Everyone." In time, I had hundreds of members and I was very happy. I truly came to love the people who were members. I found a good woman to become my wife, for my life's work. I never told anyone about my unbelief, but I was very successful getting others to seek my guidance for their beliefs. As a man of God, so to speak, giving advice gave me a great deal of satisfaction.

I needed to express the love I had for my members, so we created many programs for the people. We created a soup kitchen for the needy and the social gospel became a major theme of the church. From day care to job-training programs, we tried to see that our members were well taken care of. I had my church focus on good works and I was not sure if it was because of guilty feelings about my unbelief. I needed to do some good for my people as preaching to others what to think – was giving me what I needed – yet I wondered if what I needed was somehow evil.

I preached for many years in my church and made a good living. We stayed in a down-to-earth church and made many good friends over the years. However, I still kept my secret that I was an unbeliever. After a long career at "The Church for Everyone," I retired. Upon my retirement, my congregation gave me a testimonial dinner. About five hundred people attended, with everyone wishing me well and thanking me for being their pastor. They said that I was very influential in their lives. I was happy with my life's accomplishments, yet in the back of my mind, I thought that I was a phony. It did not faze me too much, because I was able to use my will to get people to see the world the way I wanted them to – which seemed to justify my life's work.

Many years after retirement, I was facing what I had seen many of my older members face: their deathbed. I lied on my deathbed with my family around me and I became very scared. As I was dying, I was facing the end of my life. Believing the way I did would be forever – which now seemed to be a cruel joke. However, believing that the end of life was all there was, I realized that this – in itself – is an eternal ending. I now saw and understood that there was eternal life: life after one's earthly experiences.

I had preached on the afterlife so many times yet I did not believe it. So now, I was confronted with the end of my life. I started to pray for real, for the first time in my life. I remembered the scripture that was written over the church door – which was about the "last Judgment." It said, "Come, O blessed of my Father, inherit the kingdom prepared for you from the foundation of the world." This scripture of Matthew says that doing good works such as those I helped to do with my church members – such as giving food to the hungry and drink to the thirsty, clothing the naked, visiting the sick, and visiting those in prison – are the deeds that are necessary to enter into eternal life. I realized that the good works support life – and that truly evil behavior causes the destruction of life on earth – so there must be an afterlife. I understood that the love of life – and that the understanding of God – would create eternal life for those who deserved it.

I was comforted by my life's accomplishments and doing good works – yet I prayed to God for forgiveness about my many years of unbelief. Then, I truly became a believer; I converted myself. All those years of preaching the word came rushing back to me and I realized that not only did I save others, but now my soul was saved. I felt a warmth come over me as I knew that my God had forgiven me. As my family was around my bed praying and crying as they could see me dying, I had a last tear roll from my cheek as I knew that I was being called home, leaving my earthbound family. In my last moments of life, I saw a bright white light and my being, my soul, moving toward it. My last thought was that I truly had become, "The Preacher."

The Mirror

Anna loved to sit in front of the mirror and look at herself for hours at a time. Sometimes she did not know if she loved the mirror or herself the most – as she felt that she was the prettiest girl in her neighborhood. Her mother, dad, and grandmother – all said that she was just the prettiest girl they ever saw – so it must be true. However, her mirror did not say so, like the magic mirror in the "Sleeping Beauty" story. Every day, she would say, "Mirror, mirror, on the wall: Who is the fairest of them all?" However, her mirror would not say a thing. She wished she had a magic mirror because she knew that it would tell her she was the prettiest girl in town. Yet, after talking to the mirror many, many, times – she gave up the hope that the mirror would talk to her.

One day, Anna came up with an idea. Since the mirror did not listen to her voice, maybe the written word would help the mirror talk with her. She wrote on a piece of paper the word "live" – so that her mirror would come alive. She held the word up to the mirror and suddenly saw the word "evil" looking into the mirror. Her mirror now seemed to be magic, as the word on paper spelled "live" yet on the mirror, it seemed to reverse the letters to spell "evil." The mirror was telling her to "live evil."

She knew that she was not a murderer or thief – so what was her "now magic mirror" meaning to "live evil?" Anna thought long and hard about her mirror's command. She realized that to live only for herself was seen as evil to her Christian friends. Christ-like behavior was to live for others. She now knew that her fate was to live for herself only. Not only had her mirror guided her to live this way, but it really was her nature.

Anna now wanted to come up with a plan to not only live "evil" but to show off her beautiful self. Her mother would drag her to church on Sunday and she saw her opportunity. If she joined the children's choir, she would at least be seen by all the church: recognition she desired. Anna knew she would stand out because she was so pretty. However, she discovered that she was a very good singer. She got the choirmaster to give her solos during the church service and she was applauded during the service. Anna loved all of this attention. After a time, Anna only wanted to sing solos during the service. However, the choirmaster could not do this, since there were other children in the choir. Others were getting upset with Anna's selfish ways. Soon, Anna left the choir because she knew that she was not only the prettiest – but the best singer in the choir. She would have to find somewhere else to sing to be fully appreciated.

Anna was stuck on herself. Her parents worried because she did not have any friends – which everyone needs. Eventually, her parents bought her a dog so she could have a caring relationship. Anna enjoyed the dog, as it was very affectionate to her. She would sing to her dog instead just to the mirror – and she found that the dog seemed to appreciate her singing. Anna still needed to be in the limelight, so she found some boys to start a band. She would be the lead singer. Her parents were happy she had some friends, but they knew that she was still very self-centered.

Anna still spent much of her time looking into the mirror, but her band was finding success in performing local dances. The limelight was as satisfying as looking into the mirror. Anna was very demanding of the boys in the band, which caused many arguments. However, she let it be known that she was the leader of the band and if they did not like it, they could leave. Some band members did leave, but she always found replacements. Anna took her dog, which she called, "Dog," everywhere as it was the only creature that loved her unconditionally. This protected her from all the unpleasant feelings surrounding her band. Anna spent her high school days working hard on her singing. She wanted to gain the experience she needed in order to start an actual career in the entertainment industry. Anna knew that she would become a famous singer.

After high school, she found an agent for the band, so she would be more professional. He got the band into local clubs easily because Anna was a good singer and very pleasant to look. Many gigs came her way. Anna worked very hard to try to make herself a success and she made everyone in her life cater to her every need. She became a diva early in her new career. This made the band members unhappy – yet sensing success, they put up with her demanding ego. Anna had many suitors, but she just used them to buy her things. She never cared too much for any boyfriend as it was always about herself.

Anna found herself spending less time looking into the mirror. She now had a following and many men wanted to meet her. She was truly becoming the center of attention, which she craved. Anna became increasingly famous and successful – headlining concerts and making CDs which sold by the thousands. Becoming successful, she always took the credit and spent a lot of time yelling at her handlers. She wanted to make sure everything was perfect – such as her hair, wardrobe, and stage appearance. At times, Anna was lonely, as people were around her just for the money – and they seemed to fear her. However, she could always curl up with "Dog" to get some comfort in her life.

One day, tragedy struck. Anna's dog got very sick and the vet could not help. The dog needed to be put to sleep, so it would not suffer. Anna went crazier than normal and yelled at the doctor and everyone near her – making quite a scene. Anna went to her room alone and started to cry – not only for herself, but for Dog. Anna did not want to lose her dog – but she could not be cruel to Dog. She told the vet to put Dog to sleep so he would not suffer. In her room, Anna looked hard at the mirror talking to it saying, "You told me to live evil which I did. I have become successful, yet there is emptiness in my soul," which losing her dog truly showed her.

She put her head in her hands and saw a piece of paper on the table, which she wrote lovingly DOG. Anna took the piece of paper and held it up to the mirror saying this is who I lost. To Anna's surprise, the letters seemed to spell out "God," a reversal of the letters. She now understood that her magic mirror guided her into a selfish life. Now, to get true meaning in her life, she would need to get God into her life.

Anna got in touch with her parents after not being in touch for a long time. She tried to explain how the loss of "Dog" made her realize the importance of loving relationships. Anna had all the money she needed for the rest of her life – so she devoted her career into helping those in need. She used the monies from her concerts and CDs to make sure people had good jobs so they could take care of themselves. Anna helped many, as she understood how to give unconditional love: god's love. She found the love of a good man and settled down to raise a family. Anna was committed to making others happy and she found true happiness.

Anna never told anyone about her "magic" mirror because she realized she had a strange relationship with her mirror. For the rest of her life, Anna just used the mirror to put make-up on and do her hair. After all, it was just the mirror.

Losing My Marbles

Playing marbles has always been a great deal of fun and profit for me. I played as much as I could and I played my sister in my house for practice. My sister and I just played for points because my mother did not approve of my winning and keeping her marbles; no keepsies with her. Outside of the house was a different story. I played many games and I played for keeps and won many a marble. My friends and I played in a lot creating a circle in the dirt with a stick and playing most of the day. I always came home with more marbles that I left with. Sometimes a friend would want some of the marbles he lost to me and I would sell them back to him, making a small profit. Coming home with more marbles than I left with could cause a problem with my mom so I would hide them in my bedroom. She did not like that I was beating other boys out of their marbles yet I felt I had won them fair and square.

One day my sister came to the lot and said mom was angry as I was late for dinner so I hurried home with a bigger than normal day's winnings. When I got near the house, my mom was waiting at the door so I hid my marbles in a bush so I would not get into double trouble. Well my mom was mad enough to punish me, which meant no computer for the night so I went to bed early, knowing that the next day, mom would be ok with me, as usual.

The next morning I dressed to go play and went to get my marbles, which were not in my hiding place. I screamed that someone took my marbles. I ran to my sister's room and yelled at her to give my marbles back to me as I thought she knew my hiding place. She looked at me as if I was nuts and yelled for mom. I angrily asked my mom if she took my marbles since I knew she did not like my winning them. She said no and to calm down or I might lose more than my marbles because of my attitude. I ran to my father and asked him if he saw my marbles and he said of course not and so I yelled aloud as no one knew where my marbles were.

My father looked at me and said, "Son you are really losing your marbles," and that my behavior was inappropriate and that I should behave myself. Next, I ran to the lot where my friends were and I realized that I did not get in the house with my bag of marbles. One of them must have stolen them. I knew they were jealous of my skill and I yelled at all of them to give me back my marbles that they stole. They asked me to leave until I had found my marbles as none of them would ever steal them. I ran to the police station and told them that my friends probably stole my marbles and the desk sergeant just laughed it off.

I walked home feeling sad, as I guessed I would never again see my marbles, which took so many games to win. Then, much to my surprise, I saw them. At first, I was overjoyed, but my feeling turned to anger as the poor kid on the block who we never played with – because he was poor – had them in his hand.

I yelled, "Police! The thief who stole my marbles is right here!"

The poor boy yelled with tears in his eyes, "Just because I am poor doesn't make me a thief."

I demanded, "Just where did you get these marbles," and he told me behind the bush. Wow, I thought it was my fault for blaming everyone for my forgetfulness. Now I realized that I had truly lost my marbles and I had to make it up to this boy as I was feeling a day's worth of guilt. He said if they were mine to take them. I said to make it right that "finders keepers, loser's weepers." I explained I was so sorry about calling him a thief and it was the least I could do. I asked him if I might buy the big black from him, as it was my shooter.

He said, "No," but he would give it to me if I would teach him to play marbles and to play a few games with him, I thought, "Oh, boy," I will be able to get back my lucky shooter and I will win back some of my marbles.

We became good friends and he proved to be good at marbles. My friends accepted him as he had marbles to play with and he was a decent kid. We played until the end of summer and we then went back to school. I learned a great lesson that summer in that losing my marbles: I would have to work hard to never lose my marbles again.

Hairy

I have been called Hairy all my life yet I have only one hair on my body, which is in the center of my head. The theory goes that my mother had chemotherapy because of breast cancer at the time of her pregnancy, which she was not aware of at the time. The radiation caused me not to have any hair on my body except the one on my head at birth. The doctors were amazed and made such a fuss about the condition that it made my mother see me as special – and not as a freak. The doctors fussed over me most of my life, as I was the only person on the planet who only had one hair on his body.

As a baby, the fact that I had only one hair did not seem to be much of a problem and my mother took care of the one hair. Growing up, it became more of a problem as the kids in class called me by my nickname, "Hairy." They wanted to hurt my feelings, and it did, because of the way they said my nickname. Sometimes they would sing-song, saying, "Fuzzy werezzy was a bear; fuzzy werezzy had no hair; fuzzy werezzy wasn't very fuzzy was he...," making fun of me. This not only made me angry but got me into a few fights. One day, a girl came into class who had no hair on her head because of chemotherapy. She had bone cancer and all the kids in the class understood how serious the condition was and that losing hair because of chemotherapy treatments was not something to make fun of. I now was looked upon as someone special: as the boy that only had one hair on his body and it was not a weakness. Feeling good about myself, I never wanted to put on a wig to hide the fact that I only had one hair because I was unique.

I went to college and decided to make the most of the fact that I only had one hair on my body. Many doctors and scientists wanted to study my body to understand the condition of my almost-hairless body and I made them pay me for skin samples and any other exams, which came in handy for my college expenses. I used the media to get attention as to the uniqueness of my condition. I was on many TV shows showing off my body, and did magazine interviews, which paid very well. The attention not only gained me money and a little fame but a woman who was interested in me that I someday wanted to make my wife.

The attention also had some unintentional consequences such as the hairiest personal situation I ever had to face. One night some college boys who were drunk came into my dorm room when I was sleeping and cut my hair off and left it on my pillow.
I woke up the next morning horrified thinking that my only hair had fallen out of my head. The boy who did the deed came into my room and started to laugh

at me as I was in tears. He told me he cut it off and that it should grow back, no big deal to him. Well it was a big deal to the dean, who expelled the boy from the college, because the college administrators thought that cutting off my only hair was very cruel. The hair did grow back and my girlfriend comforted me though a tough time.

I graduated from college with a degree in media, as media was very kind to me and went to work on a radio station. I married my college sweetheart and we settled down for a normal life even though I was slightly abnormal. We had a baby and my wife was so very worried that it might have my condition of being hairless. Well the baby boy was normal and had plenty of hair – for which my wife was grateful. I almost hoped for a boy with a one-hair body so I would have a son like me but I did think better of it – as being hairless really had its hard times which I did not want my son to go through.

I had a radio show called the hairy show that was a current events call-in show. One day the hairiest event happened not only for me, but also for the world. The USA, by mistake, shot off three nuclear missiles, aimed at Russian cities. Russia automatically sent nuclear warheads to USA cities. The presidents of both countries both realized that it was a mistake – and a rather big one – and they resolved that the bombs be detonated high in the atmosphere and hopefully cause no or little damage to life on the planet. I announced on air what was happing and all of the worldwide governments asked their citizens to stay indoors when the nuclear warheads were detonated. The warheads were exploded and none of the targeted cities were hit. The world was relieved. There was just one little problem: some of the radiation in the atmosphere came to earth and people worldwide began to lose their hair. On my radio show, not only did I comfort my listeners during the bomb crisis, but now I had to give advice on how to live with the trauma of having no hair.

I was just waiting and fretting about my only hair to fall yet it seemed to grow during the time. Not only was everyone else losing hair, but people's babies were being born without hair. As time went by it was becoming clear that I might be the only person on the planet with a hair on his or her body, I was truly hairy so to speak. As in college, I was used to scientists looking over my condition but now they wanted to know why I still had hair and could they clone it to create hair that would grow on other people. In college, I made money over my condition – so I decided to patent my only hair. The scientists were able to clone my hair and found that it would grow on almost everyone and so my one hair was becoming heads of hair on people's heads around the world. I was becoming rich because my hair was the only hair that was growing on anyone. It seemed that since birth, my only hair survived radiation, and the hair survived the worldwide exposure to radiation.

. My wife wanted me to try to transplant more hair on my head as the rest of the people on the world were doing – to get me a full head of hair. I almost didn't want to as I seemed to love the fact that I only had one hair as not only did it make me famous but now very rich. I found myself in the doctor's chair to try to implant more of my hair but none stayed on my head as it did with other people, I just could not grow more hair on my body. The scientists wanted to know why – but I did not want to know. I just knew that having only one hair on my head made me the hairiest person on the planet because of having trillions of my hair on other people's heads. I will truly, proudly and truthfully, be known for the rest of my life as, "Hairy."

The Storyteller

Jack just loved stories so much so – that he spent most of his time dreaming up stories during class time. Sometimes he would dream that he won the World Series with a home run. Other times he would lose the World Series with a strike out. He found his stories very entertaining – yet they landed him in a little trouble. His teachers would tell his parents that Jack was just a daydreamer, not paying attention to his studies. However, Jack's dreaming became stories to entertain his friends, making him popular. Jack's parents told him to concentrate on his studies so he could get ahead in life and that he should write down his stories, as he might want to become a writer.

Jack found that writing was not as much fun as telling stories. One time, he found a use for storytelling that he had not expected. Jack broke a dish while drying them and his mother came in and asked him angrily what happened. The cat was in the room and he told his mother that the cat jumped on the table and knocked the dish to the floor. His mother could not be angry with Jack – so she just told him to watch the cat. Jack's brother saw the entire thing and warned Jack that he would get into trouble eventually – if not with mom, then with God. Jack knew that what he had done was a little wrong but it was just an accident. He did not want his stories to be tainted, so he figured he would not use his stories to lie again – especially if his brother was around.

Jack still spent a lot of time daydreaming, which he called "storytelling to himself" – until he woke up in English Class. His teacher was telling the class about the history of storytelling. She told the class that storytelling was one of the main ways that humans communicated with each other: from caveman drawings to Greek epic poems. The class was to read <u>The Odyssey</u>, which scholars said was probably expressed through oral tradition and written down later. He was excited, as each child in the class was going to read some of <u>The Odyssey</u>, in class. After his part of reading of the poem, he knew that he really wanted to be a storyteller – but how?

His father, after listening to many a story from Jack, turned him on to a radio personality: Garrison Keillor. Mr. Keillor did a radio show called, "A Prairie Home Companion," which featured music and storytelling. The segment that Jack loved was called "News from Lake Wobegon." Mr. Keillor made up stories about people from a fictional town in Minnesota called Lake Wobegon. Jack was completely engrossed by these stories. He wanted to tell this kind of story – and thought that he could become a famous storyteller also.

Jack finished high school and went to college to major in English – to pursue writing stories. His studies were going well and he was able to get a time slot on the college radio station where he told some of his stories. He called his show "A Time for Stories" and was becoming known on campus for his show. This pleased Jack to no end. Yet there was something missing in telling a story to a microphone. There was no audience to respond to the story. Jack tried blogging some stories online to try to get responses to his stories. He enjoyed feedback he received during his short time as a storyteller. The most satisfying way to tell a story was face-to-face.

Jack continued his radio show but started a club on campus called the Storyteller Club, which became the passion of his life. He got a small group of seven people together and he told them a story and found that the others in the group in turn could tell a story of their own. Soon they became all good friends just because they told stories to each other. Some stories were very personal while others were fantasy – yet even those had some truth in them. They found about themselves and others that everyone had a story to tell. That was the way one got to know one another – and the only way to develop relationships for friendship or even love. There was many different online social media such as face book but this storytelling group felt that being in the present of each other telling ones stories was so enriching that they each went out to start their own group. The groups flourished in Jack's College and went to other colleges as Jack promoted these storytelling groups on his college radio program with the tag line that everyone had a story to tell.

73

As the college students came together, common concerns emerged such as college tuition. Many students were getting into major debt and they needed to turn to each other to try to one stop the increases in tuition and to get the governments help. Jack now understood that the stories of our life needed to be told to each other not only for love and friendship but that social problems could be addressed as people were very isolated because of the computer and being told that one needs to live for him/her self only. Jack started a web site to organize the new groups and people found their way back to each other with the seemingly lost art of storytelling. The Storytelling showed people that we are in each other's personal stories and that empathy with others grew with the growth of the storytelling clubs.

Jack went from college to public-sponsored radio. He started a successful storyteller career, which he now thought of as a public good. He promoted storytelling groups to his audience – which in turn became a national phenomenon. People discovered that they had stories to tell one other – and that they were more entertaining and more realistic than commercial entertainment. People became more social and found that they had common social needs. The public realized that the government was not addressing their needs and politicians only listened to special interest groups. They came together as a community to tell their story to the government – including needs ranging from health care to education. The storyteller clubs wanted our government to be what it's supposed to be: of the people, for the people, and by the people.

The President and congress were not addressing their priorities. The government listened only to rich people's stories and corporation's stories – leaving the people to getting poorer and poorer. Because of storytelling, people found each other and their common ground. Jack helped as much as he could, because democracy was needed to flourish. He wanted America to return to economic greatness.

One day, a representative from the Chamber of Commerce visited Jack. He told Jack that he could make a lot of money on commercial radio with his storyteller show. He could even get rich – but he would need to stop making the country restless. Jack understood what they were saying. They represented most major corporation's stories and they did not want the people's stories to be heard in government. Jack said "no thanks" to the offer and the Chamber of Commerce representative said that they had a story about him that would bring him down in the public eye.

Jack said to "bring it on" as he knew that he did not have a troubled past. The story that they had was that one snowy day he and his friends were having a snowball fight. Jack saw an old lady that used to harass him – and his friends and he threw a snowball at the lady and she fell down. They all ran away but unbeknownst to his friends, he went back to help the old woman to her feet. The troubling part of the story came out in the newspapers and the

Chamber of Commerce hoped that it was the end of "good guy Jack."

Jack, in his storytelling radio program, told the full story – and said even as a child, he felt guilty. However, he added that he was just a child. He had wanted to hit her with a snowball; but that it was just in fun – and giving her a little of her own medicine. Well, it seemed that most of his listening audience understood. Adults were children at one time – and the story did not hurt the storytelling movement.

Jack spent his time promoting storytelling by going to many storytelling groups. He traveled the country and some wanted him to run for office. However, no – he said it was the responsibility of the storytelling clubs to get men and women to represent them. This would take time because many of the current congressional representatives claimed righteous political stories. However, they were really in congress not only just for power but for the money.

Meeting many people in the storytelling clubs, he knew that the country could take a better direction. Trusting in the people, he went to the first storytelling convention. He got up at the convention and told the story of how the storytelling clubs got started. Most people knew the story, but it was a good story – and worth repeating. The people at the convention gave him the honor of his life. It was a childhood daydream-come-true – as they gave him a statue that said simply, "The Storyteller."

Sanity Clause

It was that time of year, again, where I have my fifteen minutes of fame. I play Santa Claus for my church Sunday school, which is both fun and troublesome. I hand out gifts purchased by the Sunday school teachers to their pupils, who come to me as I call their name; that is the fun part. The troublesome part is that some pupils whisper in my ear that they want to pull off my beard and expose me for whom I am, but they never have. It is a joke to them, yet if they did it in front of all the children and parents, it would not only embarrass me, but some of the little ones who really believe I am Santa – would be hurt. In addition, it is scary to see the believing ones with their wild eyes looking at me as Santa, knowing that someday they will learn the disappointing truth. There are also some so scared of Santa that they cry when I come into the room shouting, "HO, HO, HO!" I end my visit with the kids with reading, "The Night before Christmas." and leave all the children happily opening their gifts. All of the parents thank me later, for playing such a good Santa year after year. I enjoy their praise and recognition and I suspect that no one else would relish playing Santa, such is my fame.

I have wondered many times what it would be like to be really famous – which I truly believed I would love – because being a postman is not very exciting. Well, I go to church every Sunday with my family because of my wife's devotion. I am less devoted and I decided to pray to God to become famous. Many times, I prayed and nothing happened; I guess what I wanted was not that religious, yet being a good man, I did not understand unanswered prayer. So I became discouraged as the need to become famous just became stronger.

I yelled in my empty bedroom that if God will not make me famous then I will ask the devil to – and lo and behold – before me stood the devil. He said that he could make me famous and all I had to do was sell him my soul. Well I did not think twice as fame was in my eyes and I only half-believed what was going on, as it seemed to be a dream. All I had to do was sign a contract that gave him my soul and he would make me famous. The details would become self-evident, so I did and the devil vanished.

Well, almost a year passed and there was nothing on the horizon that would make me famous. I thought that not only God, but the Devil also, would not make this loser famous. Yet Christmas time was coming around again and I would again get my little bit of fame, which now seemed like fifteen seconds. A church member came up to me one Sunday morning and told me that Macys was holding auditions for this year's Santa and he thought I was good enough that I should try for it. This sounded something like the devil would do to make me famous if there ever was such a thing as a Devil. Well, I went to the audition and nailed it. They loved my, "Ho, Ho, Ho!" and the way I looked in the Santa outfit and they gave me the job. Macys' Santa: well I was coming up in the world! Very few people would know it was me, but it would be the most fame I had ever had. My family loved it and they were able to watch the Macys day parade in a luxury suite along the parade route. It was a wonderful day for me, as thousands waved to me as I went down the parade route, yelling, "Ho, Ho, Ho!" I had a hidden microphone so people all around the Santa float could hear me; it was great.

After the parade, the Macys governing board asked me if I like to play Santa next year, but with an expanded role. I said I most likely would but I needed to know the details, which they provided. They wanted me to play Santa from Thanksgiving on – around all the Macys stores – to get people in their stores to buy more. They were willing to give me a year's salary and a rent-free penthouse in NYC for a few months' work. The idea of a penthouse was a place for Macys' Santa to live, as a second home away from the North Pole. Publicity would be held in the apartment and it would decked out for Christmas, for a place from which reporters could do holiday stories. Santa publicity would also include helping some children in need and community groups under the banner of Macys in order to give Macys a good corporate name. I told my family and they loved the idea.

Holiday time came around again and we moved into the penthouse as agreed. We were introduced to the press as the caretakers of Santa and his reindeer yet all knew I was Macys' Santa except, of course, the little believers. We told the press that Santa picked us to help him because my wife had figurines of Santa from all over the world and that made it obvious to him that we had love for him. Macys gave us the figurines that were all over the penthouse; they could, of course, be purchased at Macys. We did many interviews as the caretakers and I did many Santa events in stores and community centers. Macys was pleased as store sales were up dramatically. After the Macys Christmas parade, we had our ten-month vacation and we traveled the world.

We traveled the world and met many businessmen and politicians who suggested that my Santa Claus act should be international. I was so happy to be famous around the world and I asked the Macys board if it would be possible to make Macys Santa an international star. They gave their approval as long as Macys on 34th Street was visited. My foreign and worldwide recognition would help sales. The next holiday season Macys went all out with Santa events in the USA and the major capitals of the world. It was a grand time for me, but my family was getting a little tired. After the Macys parade this year, I was asked to go to several third world countries to give gifts from people at the United Nations. Macys said I could go but it would be on my time and my family just wanted to stay at home after the busy holiday season. Therefore, I went to bring holiday happiness to children in several poor nations.

It was in South America where I had an epiphany. I fully came to understand what I was doing and what it really meant. I was glorifying myself at the expense of others. You see, when I played Santa Claus for the poor in South America, the children were happy for a day yet their parents were living on subsistence level wages while the corporations that sent me to play Santa Claus were using all their nation's resources without fair compensation. I could no longer play Santa as even in the states my role was just a way for people to spend money on toys and gifts that the corporations were selling. Even though I was famous, I really was not doing any good and I felt hollow inside. I told my handlers I would no longer play Santa, which did not bother them as they saw this Santa thing as a good thing and they would just get another man to play Santa. I went home to my house and my family – and said they would be happy to live a normal life again so I got my old job back and decided to do some actual good in the world.

There is a lot of good work that needs to be done in this world and my church led me to many projects. There was "Habit for Humanity" where I spent weekends building homes for people, which was gratifying. We had our weekly food drive where we gathered food donations and distributed to people in need. I even help my pastor visit prisoners in prisons. But what gave me the most satisfaction was that a few friends and I set up a non-profit bank to give small loans for people in South America to start-up businesses, which was successful putting to work the money that I made playing Santa Claus. I was happy being a normal person and I did not need to be famous to enjoy life.

Well, I took sick one day, I had a severe heart attack and the doctors did not think I would survive. My wife and children were by my bed and I was able to talk to them. I could tell I was dying and I did my best to let my wife and children know that I loved them very much and they held my hands and they prayed.

Just before I died, a tear rolled down my cheek as I remembered that I sold my soul to the devil and that I would not see my wife or children in Heaven – where they would surely go. I closed my eyes and my spirit left my body – and lo and behold – I was standing in front of the Pearly Gates.

St. Peter was there ushering me into Heaven and I wondered how... I asked St. Peter how I was considered for Heaven, as I had signed a contract with the devil for my soul. He laughed as he said that since I had come to my senses and done good works I could enter Heaven. However, I said what about the contract. St. Peter told me that in every Devil contract there is fine print that can bring the wayward soul back to God. I said just what could be in that fine print that would save my soul! St. Peter said the fine print is called the Sanity Clause.

Part 3: Observations

The Lover

Paul was very shy; so shy, that it was a detriment to his life. He was never able to tell any girl how he was feeling about them. He would get so nervous when he was near a girl he liked that he just put his head down and would walk the other way. He knew that he had a problem yet he was not able to tell anyone about his fears about talking to a girl that he liked. Being as shy as he was, he figured that it was just his youth and he would outgrow it someday.

In his senior year at high school, he sat next to the most beautiful girl he had ever seen. She was in his English class and her name was Eunice. He was sure she was his soul mate. Any time he started to speak to her, he became sweaty and his mouth became so dry that he could not speak. He knew that he could not carry on this way, so to overcome his shyness, he came up with a plan. He would become her secret admirer. He left her gifts at her desk when no one was in the room. He included a note said that it was from a secret admirer. She loved the gifts, which included candy and music CDs. She excitedly told her girlfriends, hoping to see her secret admirer soon.

Paul figured that now that she was receiving his gifts with joy he would be able to come out of the dark and start a love affair that would last the rest of his life. Unfortunately, his senior year in High School was coming to a close and he still was not able to express himself. He was heartbroken as she went to college and he went to work in his father's stained glass factory.

Paul learned the stain glass business and Eunice went to college to learn journalism. Paul followed Eunice on Facebook, as she accepted him as a friend. He posted very little on his page and nothing about his feelings he had for her. He still was not able to express himself but he still felt that someday they would meet and they would become lovers. She wrote everyday on her page, which Paul loved and she was proving herself to be a journalist as she was on the school paper creating headline stories.

One day, Eunice posted that her father had died and that she probably would not be able to stay in college. Her family did not have the funds for her to stay in collage. Paul knew he had to do something as he had plenty of money because he was very good at his work. He came up with a plan. He would pay for her college education but he could not do it as the secret admirer, because that would be to strange and scare her.

Paul went to the bank where she had her loan, disguised as an older man, and told the loan officer that he was her uncle and paid the loan in cash. She was then able to take out another loan to finish her college education but she never posted that an uncle paid her outstanding loan.

    Eunice finished college and got a job as a journalist with the *New York Times*. Paul thought this was great as he helped her – but now, how could he introduce himself someday? Paul had lost some of his shyness as he had been out with a few women, yet his "soul" mate, Eunice, was still in his heart. Knowing time was marching on – he knew that it would be very strange to declare his love to her. He understood that coming out of the dark could turn her off. Paul was getting up the nerve to at least Facebook her and see if she remembered him from high school. However, before he did, she posted that the job at the *Times* was ending. There was not much work for her and that she might lose her house. Paul thought that he could pay for her house but now he thought maybe he was going overboard as she did not even know that he was alive. He resolved he had to meet her and hopefully start a real relationship.

    Paul decided to just show up at her house and he brought a small stained glass window with him to use as an excuse to talk to her as if he was a salesman. Eunice opened the door and Paul said, "Stained glass man." He had with him a beautiful stained glass window with a unicorn on it. Eunice had loved unicorn pictures in high school so she invited him in. Eunice said that it was a terrific piece of glass and that she would love to own it. However, she was short of funds but asked how much he wanted.

Paul looked at the glass and at Eunice and blurted out, "I Love You."

Eunice laughed and said, "What did you say?"

Paul said, "I'm sorry but do you remember me from High School?"

Eunice pulled out her high school yearbook and there was his picture. She did remember him as the boy who sat next to her and hardly said a word. He told her that he was her secret admirer in high school and proved it by telling her he was the uncle who paid for college. She felt joy as to finally know who her secret admirer was. However, she was confused and a little scared of him. Where did he come off saying that he loved her?

He tried to explain to her how he felt and that she was his soul mate. He explained that he was so very shy during high school and that he was never able to ask her out. He knew she was in money trouble from her Facebook page and he wanted to help. He believed it was now or never to be acquainted. Eunice could see he was harmless, so she relaxed.

Eunice realized what a great story this was. She could write it up in some form and make some good money. She asked Paul as many details about his feelings for her and how many attempts he tried to tell her. Paul was very embarrassed yet it felt very good telling her all about his life, which strangely centered on her. After hours of talking, they decided to go out to dinner, which Paul saw as their first date. They had a great time together at dinner and made plans to see each other again. Eunice wanted to get this great story together which she called, "The Lover," if he did not mind. He loved the idea of her creating a story. Not only would it provide her with work, but his feelings were not seen as strange as he thought. The story helped him to normalize his feelings.

Eunice worked hard in putting this story on paper. She did not know what form the story would take: a novel, a play or serial article. Paul and Eunice became great friends and Eunice felt that she had a guardian angel watching over her. Paul paid her mortgage payment and not only was he here for her now but he was always watching out for her. Paul was very happy as his soul mate was truly becoming his soul mate. He helped with the story telling not only with his own life but by fantasying what he could have done to show his love in secret, to enrich the story.

Eunice got a break as she met a TV producer and pitched her idea of a TV show of a very shy man trying to tell his soul mate that he loved her. Every week, he would get very close to telling her but he was not able to – because of his shyness. The producer bought the idea and produced a pilot production, which the TV station loved.

The show called, "The Lover," ran for many years and Eunice created many of the story lines with help from Paul. The shows became very popular with women and gained a big audience. The show ran for four seasons. At that time, ratings declined, so Eunice and the producers decided to make the fifth season the last. The actor playing Paul would just stammer to his lover that he loved her just like Paul did. Therefore, the last two shows were about the happy couple marrying and starting a life together. The last two shows pulled a very large audience because of the marriage. Eunice and Paul, because of their love of the romantic relationship, decided to get married at the same time the actors on the last show married.

Eunice and Paul started their life together and Eunice realized how ironic it was that she was famous for creating the show, "The Lover." However, she knew in her heart that it was Paul that created their love-filled life together and she would always see him as "The Lover."

The Invisible Man

I realized that I was invisible, so to speak, at an early age. My mother would play peek-a-boo with me. She used her hands over her face to pretend that she disappeared. She then opened her hands, saying, "Boo," expecting me to laugh. Instead, I cried as I felt that I disappeared when my mother hid her face. She took good care of me, but I always felt invisible when she was away from me. The feeling of being invisible grew as I got older. The rest of my family seemed to swirl around the house, not taking much notice of me. They were not out to be mean; I was seemingly invisible because I was a very quiet kid.

It was at school that I was truly not noticed. When I was the only one who raised my hand to answer a question – and no one else did – the teacher did not see my hand. She sometimes forgot to give me test papers, as it seemed she did not see me in the back row. I was learning at school that I was so familiar looking that I was not being recognized by anyone. I could walk up to any group of kids and just listen to what was being said – as if I was not there. I figured that there must be some kind of benefit to this condition of seemingly being invisible, yet for the life of me, I could not find one.

I did start my life after my schooling. I was married and held down a job as a waiter. My troubles were that my wife hardly noticed me when I was home, and at work, I do not know how many times a customer asked for a waiter when I was standing right in front of them. I seemed to blend right into the woodwork. I needed to be recognized so I could find some contentment and joy in my life. Somehow, I needed to make it happen.

One day, I thought I had my chance. I witnessed a bank robbery and I stuck out my leg and tripped the bank robber. The police jumped on him, capturing him. It was unbelievable because nobody saw me – or thanked me. I left feeling very disappointed but determined to be recognized somehow. I was so angry that I did not care what kind of recognition I would get – even if it meant trouble. The next day, I decided to rob my bank. I walked up to the teller and gave her a bag and told her to fill it up – which she did. I then walked to the door expecting to be arrested – but no – I walked out even though there was commotion inside the bank. I went home with the money very scared.

The next day, I went back to the bank with the bag of money and saw a poster up without a picture, saying that a non-descript person robbed the bank yesterday. No one in the bank recognized me, so I went to the police station and told them, "I robbed the bank and here is the money," expecting to be arrested. They told me to sit on a bench and that they would check out my story. They thought I must be crazy. After sitting there for hours, I just walked out. However, still needing to be known in some capacity, the next day I went back to the police station. I had to tell them my story again and then they arrested me, giving me a great deal of attention.

The next day I saw a judge and I was happy that so much fuss was being made over me. Now, a government institution recognized me! I told my lawyer why I did what I did and that I had returned the money. Since I was receiving the attention I craved, I figured that all would be well. We told my story to the judge, but the judge did not believe me. The judge and prosecutor both thought that not only was I guilty – but I must have felt very guilty to come forward presenting myself and returning the money. The judge said the crime could not go unpunished so he sentenced to two years in prison. I was so scared that I almost cried. However, after the judgment everyone walked out of the court. I just followed my lawyer out into the street, a free man. After a few blocks, I tapped my lawyer on the shoulder and he said, "What are you doing here?!" I said that this is proof that I am an invisible man.

We went back to the judge and now he understood that what I was saying about myself was true. No convicted man had ever walked out of his courtroom before. He agreed that I did look very common. The judge reduced the sentence to just two years parole and told me never to try to get attention through a criminal act again – otherwise I would have to do jail time. I left scared and lonely as I did such a desperate act just to get a little attention. I realized that I needed help.

I walked to a medical building that had a psychiatrist office in order to seek professional help.

As I was walking there, I saw a community center that offered many different classes. Once class, in particular, interested me: learning to become a clown. I thought this could get me some recognition, legally. I went to the psychiatrist's office first. I saw the doctor and explained my problem of being invisible. He fell asleep listening to me so I went to the community center to see about the clown class.

I joined the class the next day and just blended in, not being noticed, until I was able to put on his clown makeup. I learnt a little about clowning such as how to fall and make it look funny. As an assignment, I had to come up with a little clown routine – which I created and called "The Invisible Man." I made believe I walked into an invisible man who got very angry and slaps me on the ground. I pantomimed that the invisible man showed no mercy slapping me around the floor. The routine ends when the invisible man sees the clown crying and has a change of heart helping the clown up and then the clown and the invisible man hug and walk off together. Well, the class loved the act and told me that I should try out for the circus. I auditioned for the circus and was hired. I was the happiest I ever felt in my life: I was being recognized – even if only as a clown.

Working at the circus, I found that I had many friends. Other clowns helped me fine-tune my act. I was billed as "Slap-Happy the Clown" because not only was I slapped by the invisible man, but also by the other clowns as they clowned around the circus rings. I was loved by the crowds. Everyone roared with laughter because my falling down was funnier than all the other clowns. There was only one problem: I was only famous as a clown – because when I took off the clown costume, I was not noticed by anyone. I decided to see the psychiatrist about this invisible problem again – but this time I would see him in the clown costume, so I would be seen.

    I went to the psychiatrist to help make some sense of my life. I told the psychiatrist my whole story and this time the doctor stayed awake. The doctor told me that he thought I felt invisible in social settings. I beat myself up, making myself believe I was a clown – and not a man to be respected. The doctor told me that I really was not invisible – and that I was just a "very common person blending in well, in the fabric of life." For some, this is not a bad thing. I thanked the doctor for the insight, as the anger I felt at people for not being recognized, was lifted from my life.

    I also realized that being recognized was not always so terrific. Perhaps it is not really so necessary in life after all. The fame I had as a clown had its pitfalls – because the children after the show not only wanted my autograph but wanted to slap me! In addition, the attention I received from robbing the bank was just wrong. Therefore, after the talk with the doctor, the insight into myself – freed me to be myself. I could now accept – and was quite content with my fate. I could now live the rest of my life as the Invisible Man.

The Dancer

Larry the garbage man had a secret: he would have loved to be a professional dancer. He lived alone, and in secret, he danced alone – always knowing that he was missing out in life because he was not dancing with a real woman. Larry felt that he was very good at dancing because he watched dancing videos and he was able to do the footsteps of many dances. As he danced, he dreamed of dancing with a beautiful woman in a grand ballroom. He was very shy around women, so at home, after he found a manikin – thrown out from a dress shop – he would dance with his make-believe friend.

He never told the guys at work of his desire because he knew that they would only make fun of him. He could dance all night and his buddies wondered why he would leave the bar after work and always go home early. They figured he was hiding something from them: possibly a girlfriend, so they decided to find out.

One night, they followed him home, without him noticing. They saw Larry go straight home, meeting no one. They decided to look into to his window – in case a person was already in his apartment. What they saw as they pulled the curtains apart was Larry dancing with a dummy, which not only shocked them, but made them want to roll over with laughter. They held off their laughter until they got back to the bar. After a good laugh at the bar they, decided to play a prank on him the next day at work.

    The next day, his buddies asked him if he wanted to meet a very nice girl; she was one of their sisters. He said, "Okay," but was afraid because girls made his hands and head sweat – and he really wanted to make a good impression in front of his buddies. Well, his buddies rolled out a dummy fully dressed up and asked him if he wanted to dance with their sister, while rolling with laughter. He was horrified and ashamed as his secret was out. Now, he knew they would never leave him alone as they were all calling for him to dance. His nickname would be "The Dancer" forever.

    One day, after the hullabaloo subsided, one of his co-workers, who always refrained from calling him "The Dancer," asked him if he wanted to meet his shy sister. He told him that his sister would dance alone in her room and he could not tell the other workers about his sister. However, he thought that Larry would understand and maybe he could come over his house one night. Well, Larry could not dance alone anymore – after his buddies found out – so maybe he should meet someone. Sitting alone at home, without dancing, was no fun.

    When Larry met Martha at his friend's house, both Larry and Martha did not have much to say to one other. His buddy had told his sister the reasons that Larry's co-workers called him "The Dancer." She knew that Larry knew that she loved to dance – and that she did it alone also. They both laughed nervously about themselves. They decided that they should try to dance together. They bought a video that showed them many dance steps and they got very good at dancing. They had a great relationship basically because of dancing. They decided to get married and were the "bell of the ball" – because their dancing at their wedding was just superb. Everyone figured that these two lonely hearts would have a good marriage as dancing would keep them always together.

One day the fair came to town and there was a dancing contest that had a $2,000 cash prize. All of Larry and Martha friends said they should enter. However, they felt shy about dancing in front of so many strangers. Their friends talked them into it and Larry and Martha did want to see how good they were against the competition. There were twenty other couples in the competition and the whole town came to see the dance competition. It was a two-night competition and Larry and Martha made it to the second round. All of their friends were there and so were Larry's buddies – who at one time laughed at him, and they were now rooting them on!

Well, as fate would have it, Larry and Martha won the competition. Everyone cheered them on but they still felt shy. They thanked their friends and went home with the money and a little trophy. Martha decided to open a little dancing school that might help other lonely hearts and Larry agreed.

Back at work, Larry's buddies now called him "The Dancer" with grudging respect and he now felt proud of his dancing. Larry realized that dancing by himself – he was a fool. However, by dancing with another – that being Martha – he could be truly and in all good spirit, be called, "The Dancer."

The Bully

I was entering high school and the worst part was that I was socially inept. I was very smart and some might call me a nerd. However, socially, I was not really smart so entering high school was scary. I had reason to be scared because on the first day of school, I walked past some very loud boys who looked like trouble – and I made the mistake of staring at one of biggest ones. He was just so scary because he looked like the strongest kid I had ever seen. He came over to me and asked me, "What are you looking at?!"

I said that I was not looking at him – but he punched my arm and said, "Don't do it again!" as his friends looked on laughing. I learned my lesson and never looked his way again. I learned to look down any time I walked past him, making his friends laugh. Through my friends, I found out that he was the biggest bully in the school and that I was just a small fish to him and as long as I stayed out of his way I would stay out of trouble with him: a comforting thought.

Half way through the school year, midterm exams were coming up and I spent a lot of time studying, not coming in contact with many kids. Then one day I went to the bathroom and there was "Billy the bully." I just dropped my books and froze in fear as we were the only ones in the room. He came up to me and said I understand that you are smart. I told him that I get good grades. He said that he did not and that he needed help in his schoolwork. Billy wanted me to help him because his father would kill him if he failed so I stuttered out that I would.

Billy also told me to keep it a secret. "No problem," I said, as I understood from his tone of voice that it was under the penalty of death if anyone found out. We spent many afternoons studying and I had to sacrifice some of my study time because I was sure I would be dead meat if I did not help him. To my great relief, he worked hard and he was learning what I was teaching: simple English and math.

One day after he got a correct answer to a tough math problem, I said, "Bully for you!" – and he punched my arm hard. He said to never call him a bully. As I was rubbing my arm, I explained that it was an English expression that meant that he did well – and that it was an expression coined by one of our Presidents. He said that he was sorry and that not only he would he not hit me again, but he would not let anyone else hit me. I gave him an education – and he would give me protection. "Fair enough," I thought.

Being hit or beaten up was bad enough – but there were guys who used words to torture me and my friends. True sadists, we thought. They would yell insults, attacking our manhood – because we were nerdish, were not popular with the girls – and we did not play sports. These attacks hurt our frail egos, which was very hurtful. Our torturers could see this – and they would laugh cruelly at us almost every day.

I told Billy about my problem. At first, he did not understand because he thought, "Sticks and stones may break my bones, but words will never harm me." I reminded him when I said, "bully" to him – it hurt him enough to hit me, so he understood and said that he would help me. He told the sadistic kids to stop bothering my friends. They did not stop until they received a few black eyes. Well, my life got better with my friendship with Billy and we remained good friends throughout our high school days.

As we neared the end of our high school days, we all wondered what to do next. I was going to a good college to major in biology – and Billy was not sure what he wanted to do. He asked for my advice. I thought that not only was he cut out for it – but it seemed that it would be natural for him to become a policeman. I told him that as a policeman he could use force to do good for the common man – similar to how he used force to do good for my friends. I told him that I was sure that he could pass all the police requirements and so he went to the police academy. We stayed in touch over the years as I went to college and received my doctorate in biology and he became a policeman.

He turned into an honorable policeman and as he matured, protecting people became his major goal in life. He never abused his power with the public; he left his bullying in high school. He understood that the bully in him was just his wild youth.

After a few years doing police work, he witnessed many officers misusing their authority. He saw too many arrested people roughed up without any just cause: just a show of force by an officer to scare the arrested person; or perhaps the officer thought the person deserved it.

Billy knew that a person was innocent until proven guilty – and punishment before a guilty verdict was wrong. What he witnessed was what many community people called police brutality and he agreed. After many incidents, he turned to me for advice as he was ready to leave the force. I thought about it and I said that police brutality is a real issue in the Police Department and that maybe he could do something about it. He wondered what and I said that the Department could use some training in "how to handle the arrested better" not only for his peace of mind but for the Department and the community.

I thought that he should ask the higher powers if he could teach in the academy – a more restrained manner of handling the arrested, which he practiced. He found the proper channels to deal with and got a job teaching in the academy: a course on the proper treatment of the arrested. He helped make the men who were becoming policemen better able to deal with justifiable force and self-control. Also, he had many current policemen come in for the class.

I knew that I was a better man knowing Billy. And, the police force was a better force because of him. I was very proud of our relationship. The only troubling thing that bugged Billy was his past. His past confronted him when we went to our class reunions as there were now fully-grown men who still had the scars from the high school bully. Even though Billy had become a pillar of the community, they would talk behind his back. Some, in fear, still called Billy THE BULLY.

The Ad Man

From my early childhood, I always seemed to be selling something. I sold papers, candy for school, and personal items for cash – such as old comic books and toys. In high school and college, friends would come to me to sell their possessions because most of them knew of my selling ability. I sold their old TVs, old computers and even an old car. I was very successful, so I figured I could sell anything. My father would say that I could sell ice to an Eskimo. I did not feel exactly that way because I never lied about what I sold and then again, I never told the total truth either. I just knew how to "razzle-dazzle" my customers. Realizing that I was not only quite good at selling but really, I enjoyed it, I went to college to learn the advertising game.

After getting my degree from college, I went to sell myself to the top advertising agency. I, of course, landed a job there – and started the very next day. I had to start at the bottom to prove myself, yet I held on to my dream that I would become "The Ad Man." The one everyone would come to; to successfully sell anything. I was put on a team to come up with an ad for a bar of bathroom soap that changed color when using it up. Thus, the user would know when to buy more soap. We called this product, "Renew." It seemed to me to be an unnecessary product, yet Renew was a catchy name for our new soap and I knew we could sell it. The soap turned blue as it got smaller so we ran TV, magazine, and newspaper ads with the slogan, "Turning blue Renew." I spent time in designing the packaging for the soap which was a white bar of soap on the box that could be peeled off to show a smaller bar of blue soap that said, "If blue, Renew."

The packaging was accepted by my team and more importantly, the public liked it. The product stood out on the shelves, getting the people to buy the soap. Because of the slogan and the packaging, the soap sold very well and I was proud of the campaign that the public seemed to love – but which I knew was just "good, old, razzle-dazzle."

One day, I saw the soap packaging on the street as garbage. I was a little disappointed since I put a good deal of thought into creating the packaging. In some ways, I thought of it as art, but then again, one might see all product packaging as garbage. I spent a few years on different teams creating ads – and having a good deal of success for many different products. Then, it became time for me to lead a team. I was just beginning to make my mark in the advertising business, when the winds of change hit the business.

There started to be an uproar of people complaining about ads. The complaints varied such as ads being untruthful – to the undue influence of adults and especially children – and selling harmful products. Congress started to create laws banning ads for products that they felt were harmful – such as tobacco, then alcohol, then fatty foods.

People were pleased because many felt like they were being manipulated into buying a product through devious means such as seeing cars traveling on empty roads, giving a sense of freedom, and after buying the car – many found road rage a major part of driving because of jammed roads. Congress finally made a law that prohibited all forms of advertising. Great, I thought: now I am without a job and career and it was the kind of work that not only was I well suited for, but I loved to do. What to do?

The next day, the law against advertising went into effect. I was cleaning out my desk and some packaging my team was working on fell on the floor and I had an idea. I ran to my boss to pitch my idea. The idea was simple as all products still had packaging on them and one could just throw them on the street so people could see the brand name. Thus, the discarded packaging would advertise the product. My boss just laughed and thanked me for the laugh as he, of course, was in a lousy mood. However, he said if I could prove my plan would move products, he would get me clients secretly, as he hated to lose his business.

I took a well-known product, M&Ms candy, and spread their wrappers in a family neighborhood. I then did the research secretly, canvassing the local stores as an M&Ms' supplier to see if more M&Ms were sold after I put the wrappers on the street. Sales went up during our trial run and my boss said that he would get on board. We would advertise in secret, even if it meant breaking the law, as he and I felt the law was very unfair.

My boss sent me to meet many clients and I pitched my idea to them successfully and they only knew me as, "The Ad Man." We signed up many clients and after a year, we had people working for us all over the country. With the wrappers, we went one step further. We put money-saving coupons on the inside wrapper, which many people took advantage of. We not only placed wrappers on the sidewalks, but we took brand new cars and placed them on the side of highways. They were placed on the side of the road as if the people were in need of assistance, but the main purpose was to show off the cars. Research showed that many people must have seen and admired the cars, because more cars were sold by the dealers in the areas in which we placed the cars. I felt that I was at the top of my game. However, it was all done in secret so I did not get any credit from society – but also no discredit from a society that banned ads. What I was doing seemed natural to my being: advertising was my life and also productive – yet it was illegal.

Well, one day it all came to an end, as I was caught in a sting operation. I went to what I thought was a new candy factory. However, federal agents posing as the factory owners signed an agreement with me to advertise their products by my placing their wrappers on local sidewalks. The agents arrested me as soon as the agreement was made. I was in trouble, but my lawyers argued that the main crime was littering. I did not know if that was true or not, but the publicity that came about with my arrest was seen by congress. The government decided to open a hearing, again, about advertising. I went to Washington to explain to the committee: the need for advertising.

When I got in front of the Congressional committee, I believed myself ready to defend advertising. I showed them the research I did with the products I advertised, which found that people responded to them in a positive manner. I told them that businesses needed to show and explain new products. Advertisements gave people a choice of many different products. Manufacturers need to show their products in a good light. I gave the example that if one plans a holiday dinner – that good presentation becomes a major part of a good meal. After I had my say, the chairman of the committee spoke to me and said that my "garbage ads" (as he called them) seem to prove that people really did not hate advertising. He added that without the advertising dollars that supported TV, radio, internet, newspapers and magazines – the cost of these items would skyrocket. His concern was exploitive advertising and I reassured him that I believed that those ads could be stopped and I would be willing to give some of my time to be on a committee to prevent exploitive ads through any new laws necessary. They thanked me for my time and the very next day congress rewrote the advertising law and permitted all advertising, that wasn't exploitive, to be allowed again.

Well, I was prosecuted only for littering – which was a small fine that my boss gladly paid – as he got back his firm. It was good to be back in business. I became a full partner at the firm and I became wildly popular as, not only had I sold ads when they were illegal, but I sold congress on allowing ads back in public life. Yes: it seems to me that I have become "The Ad Man".

Seeing Clearly

It was that time again. My eyes had become a little weaker so I needed a new prescription. I have worn glasses since I was seven years old and about once a year, I need to have my glasses adjusted for my weaker eyesight. I went to my eye doctor and had my eye exam, which showed that I indeed needed new glasses. My eyes had gotten weaker, but not so weak that I would have to worry about becoming blind. I would sometimes worry because without my glasses, everything was blurry. However, I did know from the past, that my new glasses would have me seeing clearly again.

After the exam, it was time to have fun picking out the frames for my new glasses. There were metal ones, plastic ones and all different colors, shapes and sizes to choose from. Well, I narrowed my choice down to two – and because I could not make up my mind to which I liked better, I bought both. I figured that I could not go wrong with a spare pair.

As fate would have it, the spare would come in handy as I broke one pair by sitting on them – when I left them on my sitting chair. When I sat on the glasses not only was it uncomfortable for my butt, but I felt emotional lousy. I did not know why I felt so bad, but I knew what to do: I would buy another spare pair. I went back to the eye doctor and again marveled at all the different frames and I decided to buy two more, which my doctor thought was quite enough. Yet, unbelievably, I felt a need for more.

The next day I went to a new eyeglass store and brought my prescription and bought another pair of glasses with different frames. It was the frames that were attracting me, so I told myself. Before I knew it, I had seven pairs of glasses, a different pair for every day. I wore a different pair every day, which my wife thought was very strange. I suddenly could not decide which pair of frames I wanted to wear. Well, it got worse, as at least once a week, I would buy a new pair of glasses. I had over twenty pairs before I knew it – and my wife and friends wondered about me and my collection of glasses. Even twenty wasn't enough as I bought more, telling myself that I just wanted to make sure if anything happened to my glasses, that I would be able to see clearly. My wife became worried about me and asked me to get counseling. There had to be something wrong with me and I had to agree, as I could see clearly that she was right.

I went into counseling without a clue of what was wrong with me. I had so many glasses and yet I could not see the problem. Well, I started the dialogue with the therapist about my first pair of glasses at age seven and how I felt about them. Looking back, it turns out that even though I was called "four eyes," as a child I felt mature for wearing glasses because adults wore glasses. I did remember that my family was poor and that one time I broke my glasses: the bridge of the glasses.

My father blamed me for breaking them, which I did not feel I did – even though I was bending them to make the fit better. I felt they broke because they were very cheap. He did not want to buy me another pair of glasses because money was tight and it would teach me a lesson: that I should take good care of my glasses. So, I had to glue the glasses together so I could see in school. I was reading my report in front of the class and the glue gave way and the glasses broke in two and the kids in class just roared with laughter, which embarrassed me to no end.

Well, said the therapist, "A childhood experience like this one is traumatic which stayed hidden subconsciously, until triggered by breaking my glasses by mistake."

My therapist thought I had my breakthrough and had done very good work. He thought that bringing this glasses experience to light could stop my addiction to buying glasses. I thanked him for helping me gain insight into myself and I realized that my childhood experience did cause this strange behavior. It was a great sense of relief and I no longer felt compelled to buy another pair of glasses. I left the therapist's office to face my collection of glasses, which will help me see clearly hopefully for quite a while. In addition, looking into the cloudless sky, I knew that I was truly seeing clearly.

My Golden Teeth

When I was a child, I had the experience of losing my first tooth, which I found to be a strange event. My baby teeth were being pushed out by my permanent teeth or so I was told at the time. Having a tooth fall out of my mouth scared me a little but my mom said not to worried; that a new permanent tooth would replace it. The permanent ones would see me through life and I should take care of them – as they would be as valuable as gold. She also told me that if I placed the baby tooth under my pillow at night, the tooth fairy would give me a gift as the fairy collects teeth. Well I was game for anything because I had just had a tooth land in my mouth and losing my teeth seemed just as odd.

I took my mother's advice and put the tooth under my pillow and lo and behold: I received a gift. It was a beautiful gold coin. I did not know if my permanent teeth would be worth gold but I now knew that my baby teeth were. I ran downstairs to tell my mother about the visit by the tooth fairy but thought better of it. I wanted to keep the gold coin a secret: I would hide it so no one could steal it. My mother asked if the tooth fairy had come in the night and I said, "Yes," keeping my eyes on the ground, yet out of the corner of my eye, I saw my mother smiling.

All during the summer, my baby teeth fell out and into my mouth and I received gold coin, after gold coin, which was great. I was getting permanent teeth – and rich at the same time – yet I told no one and kept my coins well hidden. One night, as I was sleeping, two teeth came out. I was expecting a good payout the next morning, yet nothing happened. I told my mother that I had been getting gifts from the tooth fairy, which was news to her. I told her my tale of woe. She laughed and said to try again as the tooth fairy was probably busy. So, I did, and two shiny gold coins were under my pillow the next morning.

Well, all good things come to an end, so I thought – as I had one last baby tooth in my mouth. This last one was stubborn, as it hung on to my gums with some skin. I was afraid to pull it out of my mouth as it might hurt and bleed. Then tragedy happened: I was running for a ball and jumping up, the tooth fell into my mouth and to my horror, I swallowed it. Now, I might not get what would have been my last gold coin. I asked my mother if I lost one of my baby teeth if I could still get a gift from the tooth fairy. She said, "No," and that the tooth fairy needed to collect teeth. It was just a fair trade that the tooth fairy gave a gift for one's teeth. Well, I decided not to be cheated so I came up with a plan!

I went to my local butcher and asked him if he had any animal heads and he said that he had a lamb's head, cheap. I bought it and went home to put my plan into action. I hammered the jaw of the lambs head until a tooth broke off. Now I had a tooth for the tooth fairy and I would not get cheated or so I thought. I put the tooth under my pillow as usual and went to sleep dreaming of gold. Well, the next morning I looked under my pillow and there it was: the lambs tooth. I was devastated. I ran to my mother and told her the whole story. Again, she just laughed and said that one cannot fool the tooth fairy. She was glad that it would be the end of the tooth fairy coming to the house and I was glad that all my permanent teeth were almost all in place. A few years later my mother told me the truth about the tooth fairy: she was the fairy. It was okay, since I was richer for the experience, and now my new teeth looked as good as gold to me.

It now became time to face the reality of my permanent teeth. I needed to take good care of them lest they get cavities and cause me pain and dental work. It came time to go to the dentist with my new permanent teeth, which he said come in straight and looked as good as gold. Even though I took good care of my teeth, some years down the road, I still got cavities and had to go to the dentist to have them filled. He gave me a choice of what to fill my cavities with: silver fillings or gold fillings. I, of course, chose gold. This way, I would truly have golden teeth. Over a number of years, I had a number of cavities and had those all filled with gold, making me a very contented young man.

Late in life, in my mid-sixties, some of my teeth needed to be pulled out – as they had become very decayed. I kept the ones with gold in them and stored them with my gold coins. The day arrived when tragedy struck as my gums went bad and no longer could support my teeth, I said goodbye to my golden teeth. Well, false teeth are rather expensive, so I took my gold coins and the gold from my teeth and turned into cash – which was more than enough for my new teeth. The gold from what I called my golden teeth let me have teeth for my golden years. Although my new false teeth were not golden, in a way, they were – because they would allow me eat normally. They might not be what I could call "my golden teeth" but they existed because of my golden teeth.

Looking Up

John and his friends, one day in the park after a baseball game, lay on the grass relaxing – and looking at the sky. They were watching big white clouds move in the sky and each of the boys, using their imaginations, saw different images in the clouds such as dogs, cats and people's faces. They tried to show each other their visions and had great fun doing so, but the clouds would break up into different shapes ruining their visions. The boys tired of the cloud game quickly and got up and went home, except John as he was fascinated by the clouds. John stayed looking at the clouds because he felt he had a new friend. In the clouds, he saw all kinds of different animals, faces and even buildings, which changed shapes – turning into different images for him. Because John's friends were not as interested as he was, John knew that he would have to find time to cloud gaze by himself.

The next day he got together with his friends for a baseball game. They were playing a tough team, so all needed to give 100% and also all the boy's families were there to watch. John played right field but he spent a lot of his time looking up at the sky for clouds. During the game, a great big cloud, almost covering the ball field's sky, interfered with the outfielders as sun streaks were breaking all around the cloud almost blinding the outfielders. As John was watching the cloud, pieces were breaking off and he imaged them as birds flying in all directions. He heard the crowd yelling but looking up he saw one of the birds was coming right at him. It looked like a dove and he ran as fast as he could to see if he could catch the cloud. He leaped and his glove went over the fence and he joyously thought he caught the dove. He fell on the ground and looked in his glove and saw he caught the ball and it was a game-ending play and they all congratulated him for such a fine catch. He never let anyone know what he thought he was doing because his friends would think him strange. John thought himself a little strange too, yet everything worked out alright.

John really felt that he had a friend in the sky and he walked the streets looking up most of the time, occasionally bumping into people. One person asked him, "Just what are you doing, young man," and he told him that he was just looking at the beautiful clouds and that he spent a lot of time doing so. The man laughed and said that John would never get anywhere with his head in the clouds explaining that phrase: that one is just wasting time, which he thought I was doing.

I still continued to look up and I saw a scary black cloud that looked like a big panther and then I bumped into another person. I turned and profusely apologized before I saw that I bumped into a very pretty girl who just giggled. I told her I was looking at the dark cloud and sheepishly said that I imagined it to be a black panther. She said she was looking at the cloud also but saw a rain goddess. I knew I found a soul mate; she said her name was Mary. It started to rain and we ran for cover and then she asked me to come over to her house.

At her house, she said that if I could get my head out of the clouds she could show me the wonders of the sky. She did so by showing me pictures of many galaxies that the Hubble telescope captured from the sky. I was truly amazed as I never saw such absolutely astounding images that were real, they sure beat my simple made-up images of clouds, yet it was still in what I called my friend, "the sky." Mary asked me if I wanted to go to the country with her family to really see the night sky. She said that the city lights block us from seeing all the stars. I asked my parents and they said yes and I was very excited: I would not only be able to sky gaze but – would do so with someone with whom I hoped would be my gal. My life was certainly looking up.

We went to the country together and hiked into the woods to a clearing and ate sandwiches for dinner. We waited for the sun to go down. As night fell, the sky shone in its full glory as there were thousands of stars. Mary and I carried a small telescope with us so she could show me some of the planets. The black velvet sky with thousands of twinkling stars was overwhelming. I must have stared into the sky without saying a word for about an hour. When I did speak, I said that I could spend the rest of my life looking up at the sky. Mary said that I could if I really wanted to but I would have to get my head out of the clouds and study real hard to become an astronomer. Then, I would be able to look up at the sky all the time.

Well, I decided that astronomy was for me and Mary wanted to write books on astronomy. We went to California's Institute of Technology and graduated with our degrees that let us do what would become our life's work: astronomy. I researched galaxies and solar system objects and Mary wrote books on my research. We were so close to one another and as our professional lives took off, as so did our love. We married and wanted to have children to share our lives with. Well the blessed day came around and Mary was to give birth. I was so nervous I passed the time in the waiting room looking for something to do. I turned to old habit: I looked out the window and watched the clouds and would you have known it, I imagined a stork flying down to me with my baby in its mouth.

It vanished just as the nurse called me into the room as Mary had given birth to a baby boy, which lifted my spirits. I realized that having my head in the clouds never wasted my time and that looking up had never let me down. Now, with my new family and a good job "looking at the sky," I would forever spend my time looking up.